IGUANAS

LIVING WILD

LIVING WILD

Published by Creative Education and Creative Paperbacks
P.O. Box 227, Mankato, Minnesota 56002
Creative Education and Creative Paperbacks are imprints of The Creative Company
www.thecreativecompany.us

Design and production by Mary Herrmann
Art direction by Rita Marshall
Printed in the United States of America

Photographs by Alamy (age fotostock Spain, S.L.), Corbis (13/Juergen Ritterbach/Ocean, B.S.P.I., Danny Lehman, Nigel Pavitt/JAI, Robert Harding Specialist Stock, Tui De Roy/Minden Pictures, Kevin Schafer, ZSSD/Minden Pictures), Creative Commons Wikimedia (Benjamint444, Leon Brocard, Michael Howard, Jongleur100, Christian Mehlführer, Los Angeles County Museum of Art, National Portrait Gallery, Luhrs Nick, Staselnik, Antony Street, Wilson44691, Peter Wilton), Dreamstime (Chwstock, Davewright321, Brian Lasenby, Mtilghma, Matilda Read, Sumikophoto), iStockphoto (qingwa), Shutterstock (Igor Alyukov, Bildagentur Zoonar GmbH, Matt Jeppson, karamysh, j loveland, Lori Martin, Kevin M. McCarthy, Nagel Photography, NagyDodo, Jill Nightingale, Matt Ragen, rebvt, Shackleford-Photography, Phumphao Sumrankong, Vikulin, Frank Wasserfuehrer, wojciech wojcik, worldswildlifewonders)

Copyright © 2016 Creative Education, Creative Paperbacks
International copyright reserved in all countries. No part of this book may be reproduced in any form without written permission from the publisher.

Library of Congress Cataloging-in-Publication Data
Gish, Melissa.
Iguanas / Melissa Gish.
p. cm. — (Living wild)
Includes bibliographical references and index.
Summary: A look at iguanas, including their habitats, physical characteristics such as their dewlaps, behaviors, relationships with humans, and their protected status in the world today.
ISBN 978-1-60818-567-2 (hardcover)
ISBN 978-1-62832-168-5 (pbk)
1. Iguanas—Juvenile literature. 2. Rare reptiles—Juvenile literature. I. Title.

QL666.L25G57 2015
597.95'42—dc23   2014028010

CCSS: RI.5.1, 2, 3, 8; RST.6-8.1, 2, 5, 6, 8; RH.6-8.3, 4, 5, 6, 7, 8

HC 9 8 7 6 5 4
PBK 9 8 7 6 5 4 3 2 1

CREATIVE EDUCATION • CREATIVE PAPERBACKS

Gish, Melissa,
Iguanas /
[2016]
33305237932342
sa   07/05/17

IGUANAS

Melissa Gish

In Panama's Darién National Park, late August storm clouds have gathered. A green iguana

dozing on a plum tree branch feels the first
raindrops on its face and opens its eyes.

In Panama's Darién National Park, late August storm clouds have gathered. A green iguana dozing on a plum tree branch feels the first raindrops on its face and opens its eyes. The iguana raises its head and yawns. Digging its sharp claws into the tree bark, the creature begins to climb upward. The iguana creeps toward an overripe wild plum dangling from a slender stem. It steps close to the fragrant

fruit and lunges for a bite, but the plum falls to the ground 30 feet (9.1 m) below. With the season nearly over and most of the fruit gone, the iguana refuses to let this plum go uneaten. The iguana descends the tree and arrives to find the plum shattered on the ground and another iguana enjoying the feast. Eyeing each other calmly, both lizards fill their mouths with bites of the juicy, red fruit.

WHERE IN THE WORLD THEY LIVE

■ **Galápagos Land Iguana**
Galápagos Islands

■ **Galápagos Marine Iguana**
Galápagos Islands

■ **Fiji Iguana**
forests of Fiji and Tonga

■ **Chuckwalla**
deserts of southwestern U.S. to northern Mexico

■ **Desert Iguana**
Sonoran and Mojave deserts

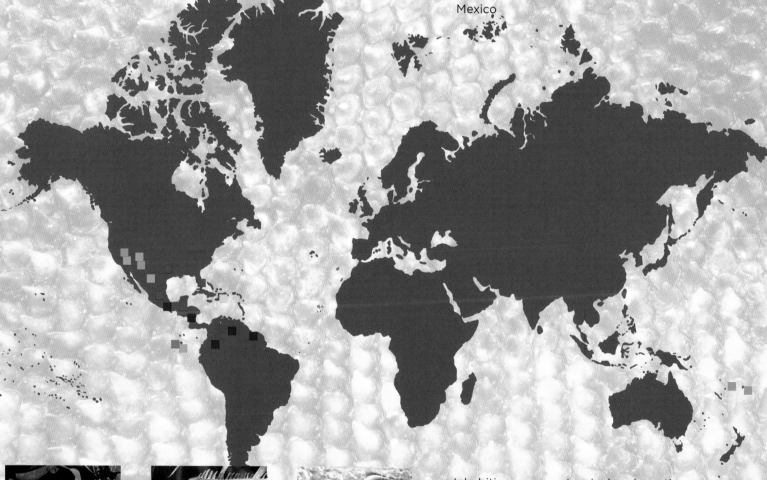

■ **Spiny-tailed Iguana**
Central America and southern U.S.

■ **Green Iguana**
Central and South America

■ **Rock Iguana**
West Indies

Inhabiting warm or tropical regions, the approximately 40 species of true iguanas are often organized into 8 groups: chuckwallas, Galápagos land, Galápagos marine, Fiji, desert, spiny-tailed, green (or common), and rock iguanas. The colored squares represent areas in which members of the eight iguana groups can be found today.

O f the more than 5,600 different lizards, about 800 are included in the family Iguanidae, and only about 40 of those are members of the subfamily Iguaninae, or true iguanas. Scientists have disagreed on the classification of some iguanas and related lizards but generally divide true iguanas into eight groups: Galápagos land, Galápagos marine, and Fiji iguanas, named for their geographical locations; chuckwallas; and desert, spiny-tailed, green, and rock iguanas. These iguanas all came from a single common ancestor older than the first dinosaurs, making them some of Earth's most ancient creatures. The word "iguana" is derived from the name given to iguanas (*iwana*) in the West Indies by the **indigenous** Arawak people. When Spanish explorers arrived on the islands in the 16th century, they wrote accounts of *iuannas*—the islands' iguanas, which they found very tasty.

Iguanas inhabit a variety of Southern Hemisphere environments. Galápagos marine iguanas live on nearly all the Galápagos Islands off the coast of South America. Three species of Galápagos land iguanas are found on

Male marine iguanas show off vibrant colors during mating season, which can last from December to March.

The critically endangered Utila spiny-tailed iguana is the only iguana species that lives in mangrove swamps.

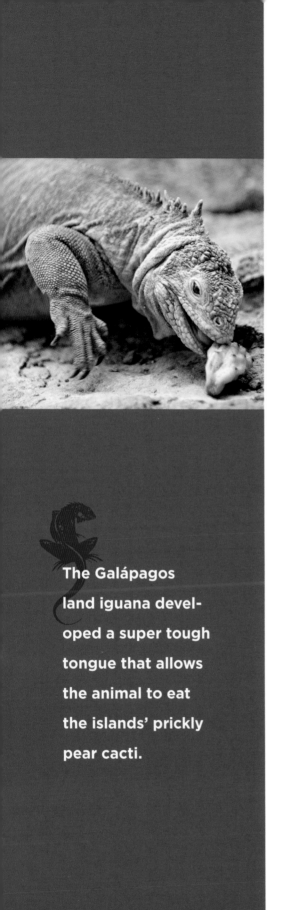

The Galápagos land iguana developed a super tough tongue that allows the animal to eat the islands' prickly pear cacti.

just six of the islands. The Fiji iguana makes its home on the island for which it was named as well as the island of Tonga, where humans introduced it. Chuckwallas are found throughout the southwestern United States, northwestern Mexico, and various coastal Pacific islands. Desert iguanas live in the Sonoran and Mojave deserts, and spiny-tailed iguanas are found from Mexico to Central America. Green iguanas, also known as common iguanas, are native to the forests of Central and South America and the Caribbean Islands, though **feral** populations now exist throughout the far southern U.S. and Hawaii—the result of people releasing pet iguanas into the wild. Rock iguanas are found only in the West Indies.

Iguanas are reptiles. Reptiles are ectothermic animals, meaning that their bodies depend on external sources of heat, and their body temperatures change with the environment. Iguanas must warm their bodies in the sun. If they get too warm, they retreat to shade to prevent overheating. One species, the Galápagos marine iguana, cools itself by spending much of its time in the water. Iguanas are diurnal, meaning they are active during the day and sleep at night. When an iguana sleeps, it closes its

Like the bald eagle in America, the
endangered Fiji banded iguana is
considered a national treasure in Fiji.

A healthy iguana has a soft, flexible dewlap, but a sick iguana's dewlap may become stiff and dry.

eyelids from the bottom up. While the iguana is awake, a see-through inner eyelid called a nictitating (*NIK-tih-tayt-ing*) membrane remains closed over each eye, providing protection from dust and debris.

Iguanas have dry, scaly skin and one row of spines on their back that extends from the neck to the tip of the tail. A flap of skin called a dewlap hangs under the chin. The dewlap is small in young iguanas but grows larger with age. Females have smaller dewlaps than males, whose dewlaps can be long with folds like a fleshy curtain. The dewlap serves various functions. It may be extended when an iguana is cold and wants to absorb extra heat or is hot and wants to catch a breeze. The dewlap is also used in iguana communication. Larger scales around the back of the neck form what is called the dorsal crest. The flesh of the dorsal crest is fatty with few nerves—similar to the tissue of human earlobes. Iguanas have pouches of muscle under the jaws called jowls. Both male and female iguanas have jowls, but in mature males, the jowls grow large. Femoral pores, which are spots that secrete a scented bodily oil, line the inner thighs. The pores are larger on mature males than females. The size of

Enlarged pupils (the black center of the eyes) indicate that an iguana may be curious about something it sees.

Most iguana species can regrow a broken tail within two to eight weeks, though its color and shape may change.

Iguanas store fat in their necks and tails and under their jaws, while their bodies and legs are very muscular.

the jowls and femoral pores are what set males apart from females in most species.

Iguanas have muscular legs with five clawed toes on each foot. The sharp claws provide grip when climbing over rocks and up trees. Like most reptiles, iguanas reproduce by laying eggs. The largest lizards in the world, Komodo dragons and other monitor lizards, can grow to more than 10 feet (3 m) in length. Not far behind is the green iguana, which can grow to roughly 7 feet (2.1 m) from snout to tail and weigh as much as 20 pounds (9.1 kg). The heaviest iguana is the Grand Cayman blue iguana (a species of rock iguana). Despite being about 2 feet (0.6 m) shorter than the green iguana, the blue iguana can weigh up to 30 pounds (13.6 kg). The Galápagos marine iguana, which is representative of most iguana species, grows to about 2 feet (0.6 m) in length, while the Yucatán spiny-tailed iguana, the smallest iguana species, reaches no more than 10 inches (25.4 cm) in length.

Iguanas' closest relatives are members of the seven other subfamilies in the family Iguanidae, including the anoles and the collared, horned, and ground lizards. Unlike most other lizards, which are carnivorous, or meat-

eating, iguanas are herbivores. Their diet consists almost exclusively of plant matter. While iguanas may accidentally ingest an occasional insect or slug while browsing on vegetation, they do not actively hunt prey. Iguanas' hunger is satisfied by fruits, flowers, leaves, moss—even fungi. Marine iguanas eat mainly seaweed and algae.

Iguanas do not chew their food. Rather, they use their razor-sharp teeth to sheer off mouthfuls of vegetation.

Because iguanas do not chew their food, they prefer soft fruits and vegetation that can be easily swallowed.

An iguana might lick its tongue on the ground to determine the different scents of food, predators, and mates.

As iguanas grow, they gain teeth, eventually boasting as many as 120. When old teeth wear down, they fall out and are replaced. Each tooth may be replaced up to five times a year. An iguana will go through several thousand teeth in its lifetime. The iguana's thick tongue is used to push food to the back of the throat. Then mucus produced by the **esophagus** makes the food slippery. The esophagus contracts to work food down into the stomach, where stomach acids break down the material before sending it on through the digestive system.

Because iguanas eat plant matter, their digestive system is different from that of other lizards. Iguanas have a body part called the hindgut between the small and large intestines. It is filled with microscopic organisms that break down plant fiber. In order for these organisms, called microflora, to survive and do their job, an iguana's body temperature must be at least 85 °F (29.4 °C). The **nutrients** extracted in the hindgut provide up to 40 percent of the energy that an iguana gets from its food. If an iguana's body temperature dips below 85 °F, microflora can't break down plant matter, and the animal can be in danger of starvation.

Predators such as great blue herons represent constant threats to marine iguanas' survival.

To escape a predator, the green iguana may leap from its perch high in a tree into a pond or stream below.

Marine iguanas can remain underwater for up to an hour while feeding, after which they usually bask in the sun.

MOSTLY MELLOW

I guanas typically live 15 to 20 years in the wild. Captive iguanas can live to be 30. Most iguanas are calm by nature and gather in social groups. Hundreds of individuals make up marine iguana colonies—the largest iguana social groups. Iguanas bask together and even climb over each other, usually without any conflict. Only during mating season do male iguanas become aggressive toward one another. Depending on the species, iguanas reach maturity at different ages. While green iguanas are ready to mate as soon as they are 18 months old, rhinoceros iguanas of Haiti and the Dominican Republic do not mature until they are 5 years old. Tropical species, such as green iguanas, mate from November through May, but desert species, such as chuckwallas, **hibernate** in winter and mate from April to July.

The biggest, strongest male iguanas establish dominance by chasing away weaker males from an area. The boundaries of this territory are then marked with a smelly, oily substance secreted from the femoral pores on the male iguana's inner thighs. Fights over territory are common, with combatants clawing and biting each other

Fights between territorial male iguanas typically begin with bites to the highly sensitive jowls.

Depending on their size, marine iguanas can swim up to 1 mile (1.6 km) per hour and dive up to 50 feet (15.2 m).

Female iguanas may be receptive to mating only a few days a year—otherwise, they try to chase away interested males.

until one gives up and moves on. To attract females to its territory, a dominant male goes through an elaborate courtship ritual that includes head bobbing, extending and fanning the dewlap, and rocking the body from side to side. Females that enter a territory are also marked with the dominant male's scent.

Iguanas are polygynous, which means dominant males will mate with a number of different females, forming no bonds with any of them. When a dominant male's attention is on one female, other males called periphery males (because they linger on the edges of a dominant male's territory) will take the opportunity to pursue other females. Young males may even try to trick their way into mating. Called sneaker males, these young males sneak into female groups by posing as females. They do not display male behaviors until the dominant male's back is turned—then they sneak up on nearby females and quickly mate with them.

A female iguana does not eat much in the weeks before laying the eggs that have been developing.

After mating, fertilized eggs begin to develop inside the female's body. The number of eggs varies by species and size. Green iguanas may produce up to 70 eggs, while blue iguanas rarely produce more than 20. Older and well-fed iguanas produce more eggs than younger and undernourished iguanas. Depending on the species, eggs may take from 59 to 84 days to develop. When the time comes to lay the eggs, a female will use her claws to dig a nest in the ground. If space is limited, several females may share a nest, which can be up to three feet (0.9 m) deep. After depositing a **clutch** of leathery eggs, the female covers the nest with soil, sand, leaf litter, or whatever is available. Some species may guard their nests for a short time, but most iguanas simply walk away and never return. With the summer's heat at its peak, the eggs will be

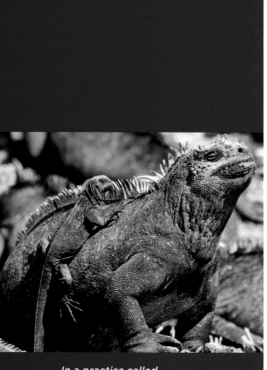

In a practice called coprophagy, hatchlings eat adult iguanas' waste to establish bacteria that aids in digestion.

Even reptile specialists cannot determine the gender of most iguana species by appearance until the lizards become mature.

incubated in the ground. Predators, temperature changes, and other factors affect eggs. In many species, only about 35 percent of a clutch survives long enough to hatch.

As a baby iguana grows inside its egg, an egg tooth develops on the tip of its snout. This sharp projection of skin enables the hatchling to slice through the egg's leathery interior lining and break the shell. The egg tooth either falls off or is resorbed into the body within a week of hatching. All the hatchlings claw their way out of the nest at the same time. For most reptiles, the temperature inside the nest determines the gender of the offspring, with higher temperatures producing more males. However, iguanas are the exception to this rule, with a clutch of eggs producing a random mix of males and females that all look like miniature versions of their mothers. The males will not develop the characteristic large jowls or femoral pores until they mature. In the case of the Fiji iguana, the young are dark green upon hatching but lighten to emerald green and develop whitish bands and spots over their backs within a few hours. Males develop larger bands as they mature.

Like all reptiles, iguanas must shed their skin as

Shortly after hatching, young iguanas grow quickly and shed their skin often during their first several months.

Unlike snakes, which shed their skin in one piece, iguanas and most other lizards shed in flakes.

they grow because reptilian skin does not stretch as the creature develops. As soft, new skin grows, iguanas often rub themselves on rocks or branches to aid the removal of old, dry skin. Depending on the species, this renewal process occurs up to four times a year throughout an adult iguana's life. Iguanas may exhibit color changes over their lifetimes as well. Green iguanas often turn brown or gray with age, while male marine iguanas may turn orange during mating season. The Fiji iguana has the ability to change its color at will, darkening its green so that its white bands stand out. This appearance is meant to chase rivals away from a territory.

Except for occasional hissing, iguanas do not vocalize. They communicate using body language. To convey calmness and control of their personal space, iguanas slowly bob their heads up and down at each other. If an iguana is being pestered, however, it may become angry. An agitated iguana will vibrate its head from side to side while bobbing it very quickly. This tells other iguanas to back off.

When iguanas first encounter each other, they may quickly pop out their dewlap in a gesture that says, "Hello, I'm not afraid of you." An iguana that is afraid of something—a predatory hawk or an aggressive male during mating season—will fully extend the dewlap, turn so that the side of its body is facing the offender, and stand up tall on its legs. This posture makes the iguana appear larger. Opening its mouth in a wide gape to reveal its bright pink tongue and sharp teeth further gives the impression of ferocity. Iguanas even nip at each other as if to say, "Move out of the way," and whip their tails at each other when they want to hurry others along.

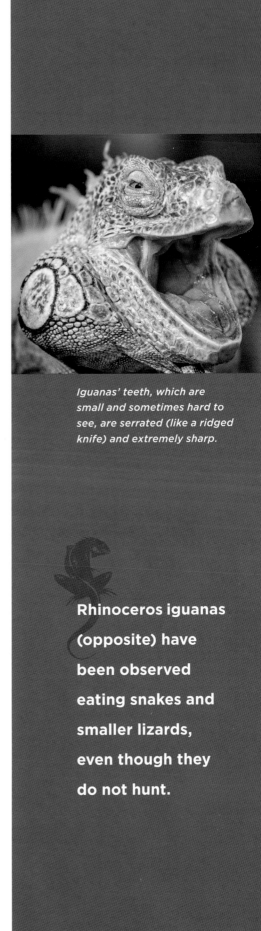

Iguanas' teeth, which are small and sometimes hard to see, are serrated (like a ridged knife) and extremely sharp.

Rhinoceros iguanas (opposite) have been observed eating snakes and smaller lizards, even though they do not hunt.

The Guna people of Panama are known for their stylized fabrics, which often contain images of iguanas.

Ceramic pottery from Colima, Mexico, most often featured dogs but also portrayed animals such as iguanas.

R eptiles are common symbols in the **cultural** history of many native peoples of the Americas. For example, the ancient peoples of **Mesoamerica** included the iguana in their traditions and **mythology**. Pottery featuring images of birds and reptiles—including iguanas—was found in central Panama and is approximately 4,000 years old. Discoveries made at Sitio Conte, an archaeological gravesite in Panama, are dated to the 5th century A.D. and depict iguanas, boa constrictors, and caimans (small crocodile relatives) on bowls that may have been used in funeral rites.

Many iguana **superstitions** have persisted over the centuries. They are typically the result of generations of storytelling. Even today, some people in Barbados believe that seeing an iguana inside a house predicts the addition of children to a family. In southern Dominican Republic, superstitious farmers believe that evil iguanas purposefully run underneath farm animals, using their sharp spikes to rip open the animals' bellies. On the Caribbean island of Bonaire, some people believe that iguana soup is a love potion.

The Andros Island iguana is endangered because feral pigs regularly dig up iguana nests and eat the eggs.

The critically endangered Fiji crested iguana has the ability to rapidly change color from green to black when threatened.

In Costa Rica, myths tell how a god named Sibo created all the humans and animals from grains of corn. In one story, Sibo heard a cry for help and told the iguana, who was lounging in the sun, to go investigate. The iguana, feeling very comfortable and lazy, refused to go. Sibo was angered by the iguana's disobedience and beat him, which explains why the iguana has bumps all around his neck and head. Sibo then threw the iguana into the river to drown him, but the iguana played dead until Sibo went away. Then the iguana hurried into the treetops, where he remains hidden to this day.

The ancient Mbocobis people of Paraguay believed the tallest tree in the forest was a World Tree, which held up the sky like a pole holding up a tent. The Creator peeled a piece of bark off the World Tree to make the iguana. A myth told by the Kuna, descendants of early Panamanian Indians, involves two powerful gods: Tad Ibe, a sun god, and Iguana Chief, a jungle god. The two had a fierce battle over who should rule the world. Tad Ibe emerged the winner and transformed Iguana Chief into the green iguana. To get back at the sun god, the iguana stole fire from him and gave it to humans. But humans used fire to cook

meat and hunted iguana down for food. To this day, the Kuna make iguana meat a regular part of their diet. In many parts of Central and South America, green iguanas are called bamboo chickens because they live in trees and are timid and easy to catch—and they taste just like chicken!

In North America, the indigenous peoples of the Southwest included chuckwallas in their rock art. Many desert-dwelling tribes also ate chuckwallas. Because these lizards would wedge themselves deep inside rock crevices and puff up to keep from being pulled free, hunters would use long, sharp sticks to poke the chuckwallas—in

New Mexico's Three Rivers Petroglyph Site protects more than 21,000 glyphs throughout 50 acres (20.2 ha) of desert.

THE CHUCK-WALLA SPEAKS

The Chuck-Walla is born of the desert, where the mountains dip into Death Valley; where vegetation ceases to grow; where the land is made of sand and borax the Chuck-Walla lives and flourishes. The heat-baked rocks of the Funeral range, the ledges of ore and malapi, the sagebrush and greasewood all contribute to its existence. Among these elements the Chuck-Walla is at home. It is a part of the desert, always has been and will continue to be while the rocks last and the sun shines.

This is a tip on the low down. Don't be an Indian. Don't try to dislodge the animal. A pull and a copper wire won't do the work. The Chuck-Walla has a purpose. It may seem that its chief business in life is to bask in the sun, catching flies the while, or scratching a hole in the sand to expose a new vein of copper. If so, that's the Chuck-Walla's concern just so it catches the flies successfully and scratches with energy at the hidden lodes.

Like other creatures of the desert the Chuck-Walla is guided entirely by instinct. It does what it lists and what to it seems right, making no apologies, giving no accounting, except to its Creator, never lifting its tail to wave as a sign of distress. It fights its own battles in its own way. It is no hypocrite. It may amuse the initiated and startle the uninitiated, but once it has taken its stand it cannot be changed. The size, power or dignity of its tormentor will carry no weight. If necessary, the Chuck-Walla will bite, and this bite is not pleasant. But withal the Chuck-Walla loves to bask in the sun and live a life of peace. Watch it in its wallow, leave it unmolested, be amused by its weird and surprising antics, and let it go at that, if you are wise.

excerpt from The Death Valley Chuck-Walla, *by the Chuck-Walla Company (1907)*

essence, deflating them. Then the hunters used hooked sticks to drag them from their hiding places. Chuckwallas were either eaten raw or cooked over hot stones. Some tribes, such as the Havasupai of the Grand Canyon, did not hunt chuckwallas. They believed killing a chuckwalla would bring bad luck to the entire village.

Contemporary stories about iguanas can be found in comics and on television. The Iguana is a supervillain in the Spider-Man comic world. Created by Bill Mantlo and Jim Mooney, the Iguana's story was first told in 1979. According to the comic, Dr. Curt Connors is a scientist who transforms into "The Lizard." While researching the ability of certain reptiles to replace missing limbs, Connors performs an experiment on an iguana named Iggy. When the experiment goes wrong, Iggy is transformed into a human-sized iguana-man with super strength and the power to control the minds of other reptiles.

A less dangerous iguana is Jub-Jub, a green iguana that has appeared occasionally on the animated television series *The Simpsons* since 1993. Jub-Jub belongs to Selma, the Simpson children's aunt. Selma treats Jub-Jub like her child, hugging him and spoiling him with treats. Another

A stamp printed in the Southeast Asian country of Cambodia around 1987 featured a chuckwalla.

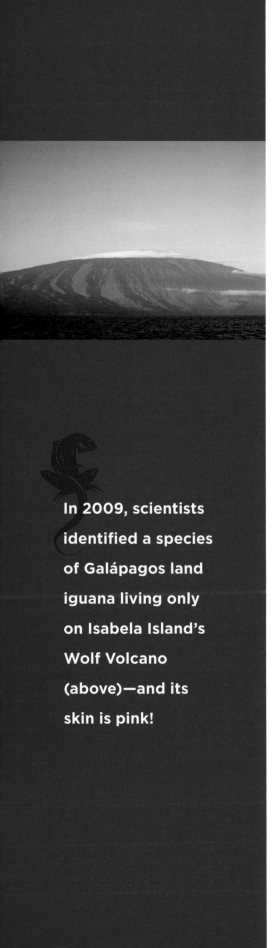

In 2009, scientists identified a species of Galápagos land iguana living only on Isabela Island's Wolf Volcano (above)—and its skin is pink!

cartoon iguana appears regularly in Bill Amend's *FoxTrot* comic strip. *FoxTrot* features the Fox parents and their three children—Peter, Paige, and Jason—plus Quincy, a hungry iguana with a nose for trouble. Jason trains Quincy to not only chew up Paige's clothes and toys but also to spit the mess onto Paige's bed. Jason sometimes tosses Quincy at Paige's face. Despite being caught in the middle of the Fox family's sibling rivalry, Quincy enjoys life and often imagines himself as a gigantic lizard tromping through a terrified city. Quincy's dream sequences are based on what is perhaps the best-known iguana of all time: Godzilla. Created in 1954 by Japanese movie producer Tomoyuki Tanaka, the upright-walking, fire-breathing, city-stomping iguana monster's debut movie was called *Gojira*, pronounced *go-ZEE-dah* in Japanese.

American moviemakers edited the original movie and renamed it *Godzilla, King of Monsters!* in 1956. Since then, more than 30 Godzilla films have been made in Japan and the U.S.—the most movie sequels in history. Godzilla is said to be between 164 and 328 feet (50–100 m) tall. Tanaka once commented that Godzilla was meant to be a cross between a *Tyrannosaurus rex* and an iguanodon—a

dinosaur named for its resemblance to the green iguana. Despite the destruction he causes, Godzilla always manages to protect humans from much worse monsters than himself, including Ghidorah, a winged, three-headed dragon; Mothra, a giant moth that shoots death rays; Rodan, a flying dinosaur that creates hurricane winds; and Ebirah, a giant lobster that destroys ships. The 2014 *Godzilla* explains Godzilla's origins.

A Godzilla statue stands near Ginza, the Tokyo neighborhood that Godzilla destroyed in the 1954 movie.

Most dinosaur remains are little more than teeth or bone fragments, but occasionally, complete skeletons are unearthed.

PESTS, PETS, AND PERIL

T he first known iguana ancestor was *Palatodonta bleekeri*, a small, armored dinosaur that lived about 246 million years ago in shallow water. It was potentially four feet (1.2 m) long and had two rows of teeth on its upper jaw and one row on its lower jaw—perfect for crushing the shellfish that made up its diet. As it **evolved**, some of its descendants moved onto land and lost their armor, becoming lizards, while others remained in the ocean and developed larger shells, becoming sea turtles.

In 2012, a group of **paleontologists** from the University of California, Berkeley, found the jaws and teeth of a previously unknown iguana ancestor. *Barbaturex morrisoni*, a 6-foot-long (1.8 m) and 60-pound (27.2 kg) lizard, lived in what is now Southeast Asia about 37 million years ago. Despite being larger than the carnivorous mammals that shared its habitat, this lizard was not a hunter—its fossilized teeth indicate it had evolved to become herbivorous. Iguanas continued to spread around the globe, evolving to cope with either desert or rainforest environments while avoiding cold

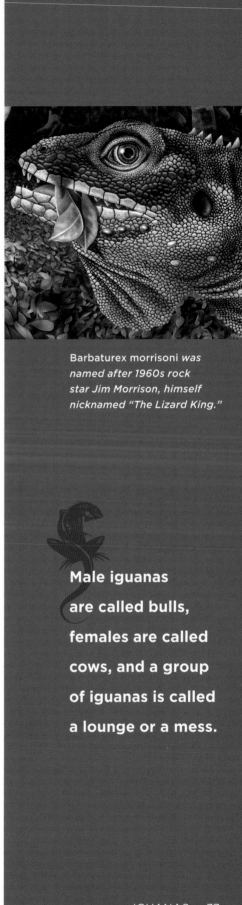

Barbaturex morrisoni was named after 1960s rock star Jim Morrison, himself nicknamed "The Lizard King."

Male iguanas are called bulls, females are called cows, and a group of iguanas is called a lounge or a mess.

Charles Darwin spent only five weeks on the Galápagos Islands, but his research altered the course of science.

climates. About 10 million years ago, in what are now the Galápagos Islands, some early iguanas returned to the sea, evolving into the modern marine iguanas.

In 1835, Charles Darwin visited the Galápagos and first encountered the Galápagos marine iguanas. He wrote in his journal that the iguanas were not afraid of him, so, in addition to cutting them up to find out what they ate, he conducted a number of simple experiments on them. To find out how well they could swim, he picked them up and threw them as far as he could out to sea. They usually swam back to shore. He also tied rocks to them and dropped them into deep water to see how long they could remain alive. He discovered that the iguanas could survive for only about an hour before drowning. Since Darwin's time, science has become more controlled and precise.

Today, only scientists with special permits are allowed to set foot on most of the islands in the Galápagos archipelago. The Galápagos marine iguanas are the only water-dwelling **aquatic** lizards in the world, and the country of Ecuador, which controls the Galápagos Islands, considers them a national treasure. Some studies

involve the iguanas' **adaptations** to life on various islands. On some islands, the iguanas are small—from six to eight inches (15.2–20.3 cm) long—while on other islands, the iguanas approach seven feet (2.1 m) in length. Research shows that iguana size is directly linked to food supply. Where food is more abundant, the iguanas are bigger.

Global **climate change** is having an effect on marine iguanas. German scientists who collected data in the 1990s shared their findings with researchers from Yale University in 2004. The researchers found that, as weather patterns shifted in ways that affected food supplies, the iguanas

Though mostly protected, the Galápagos Islands host roughly 180,000 visitors to 45 approved sites annually.

*Despite conservation efforts,
the Grand Cayman blue iguana
will not survive in the wild
without further help.*

were able to adapt. Scientists believe that iguanas secrete a **hormone** that allows them to actually change size from year to year. The changes are slight but measureable— iguanas' bones become less or more dense and can thus carry less or more body weight. This adaptive ability has allowed marine iguanas to survive for millions of years. And because the Galápagos is a protected habitat where adult marine iguanas have no natural enemies, this iguana species' population is considered healthy and stable.

Not all iguana species are as fortunate. Farmers on the islands of Barbaretta and Roatán, off the coast of Honduras, consider the Roatán spiny-tailed iguana a pest because it frequents cropland and orchards. These iguanas are often killed, despite being listed as endangered on the Red List of Threatened Species that is published annually by the International Union for Conservation of Nature (IUCN). In addition, habitat loss due to land development has devastated populations. Fewer than 2,500 mature Roatán spiny-tailed iguanas are thought to exist. While conservation efforts are underway, the iguana is given no legal protection and is thus vulnerable to continued persecution.

An iguana that does enjoy legal protection is the Grand Cayman blue iguana, which lives only on the island for which it is named. In 2002, the Blue Iguana Recovery Program found that only 10 to 25 blue iguanas remained in the wild. Located at the island's Queen Elizabeth II Botanic Park, the program has played a major role in blue iguana conservation. **Captive-breeding** and housing young iguanas until they are big enough to survive in the wild have helped the blue iguana's

The black spiny-tailed iguana is the world's fastest-running lizard, reaching speeds of 21.7 miles (35 km) per hour.

Captive iguanas permit being handled by their owners only because they associate them with food.

The White Cay iguana became the most endangered lizard on Earth when rats introduced to the Bahamas devoured the iguanas' eggs.

numbers recover. Nearly 800 blue iguanas now live in 3 protected habitats on Grand Cayman Island. The program encourages people to learn more about these iguanas by visiting their Facebook fan page.

In some parts of Central America, green iguana populations are declining. Green iguanas suffer from overhunting and the pet trade. Nearly a million green iguanas are imported to North America each year to become pets. Experts emphasize, however, that only experienced reptile enthusiasts should own iguanas because they require a specialized diet, regular care such as nail clipping and skin conditioning, and plenty of space to stretch out their bodies. While they can be tamed, pet iguanas go through periods of aggression and need to be handled carefully during mating cycles—whether they have access to a mate or not. Bites can require numerous stitches, and most iguanas carry salmonella, an intestinal bacterium that can be spread to people. Iguanas and their cages must be kept very clean because salmonella can be deadly to humans.

While they are some of the most ancient creatures on Earth, many iguana species are now perilously close

to **extinction** as they struggle to cope with challenges such as habitat loss, global climate change, and predation by dogs and cats introduced to once predator-free islands. Education and conservation efforts such as those made by the American Zoo and Aquarium Association Rock Iguana Species Survival Plan, led by Chicago's Shedd Aquarium, and the Nicaragua Iguana Project at Nicaragua's Lost Canyon Nature Reserve are valuable. However, much more work needs to be done in order to make a lasting difference in the lives of iguanas on Earth.

If the environment is too dry while an iguana is shedding, its spikes may be in danger of breaking off.

ANIMAL TALE: IGUANA INVADES THE LAND

For 2,000 years before the 1499 arrival of Spanish explorers in what is now northern Colombia, the Tairona people lived on an isolated mountain range called the Sierra Nevada de Santa Marta. Tairona spiritual leaders, called *Mámas*, were charged with maintaining *yulúka*, or harmony in the world. The following myth, told by the Kogi people (descendants of the Tairona) recounts how the iguana challenged this harmony.

In the old days, the animals of the sea stayed in the sea, and the animals of the land stayed on the land. To maintain *yulúka*, or harmony, the *Mámas* kept all the creatures in their proper places. But not everyone was content living in their separate places. Two animals, in fact, were very unsatisfied with their places in the

world: Heiséi ni, an enormous sea monster, and Mákto, a timid opossum.

One day, Heiséi ni went to see Shimarúa, a great *Máma*. "I wish to leave the sea," he said. "I am bored there. I have hunted all the greatest creatures and taken my place at the top of the sea's chain of life. I wish to move onto land now."

"Impossible," Shimarúa said. "The land has just enough great predators: Nab, the jaguar, and Namsàui, the anaconda. They are at the top of the land's food chain. There is no room for others."

Heiséi ni wished he could come onto the land and hunt these two marvelous creatures. What a challenge it would be! He begged, but Shimarúa told him, "Go back to the sea and be satisfied with your place in the world." Heiséi ni did as he was commanded.

The next day, Mákto went to see Shimarúa. "I wish to leave the land," he said. "I am scared here. I am constantly afraid of being eaten by the larger animals as I scavenge for food. If I went to the sea, I could hide on the sandy floor and eat plenty."

"Impossible," Shimarúa said. "The seabed has enough creatures. There is not enough food for more. Go back to the forest and be satisfied with your place in the world." Mákto did as he was commanded.

Heiséi ni and Mákto remained restless. Risking Shimarúa's anger, they traded places. Heiséi ni climbed onto the land, and Mákto scurried into the sea. Heiséi ni immediately hunted the jaguar and the anaconda. He ate up nearly every one of them. Without jaguar and anaconda to hunt the smaller animals, soon there were too many creatures and not enough food for them all. The land's harmony was terribly unbalanced. Meanwhile, Mákto scuttled along the seabed eating all the food he could find. Soon, there was not enough for the other scavengers. The sea's harmony was dreadfully unbalanced.

Shimarúa was furious. He could repair the damage, but he wanted to teach Heiséi ni and Mákto a lesson. So he transformed Mákto into the Caribbean reef shark and forced him to work hard day and night hunting for his food. With a mighty predator in the sea once again, the sea's harmony was restored. Then Shimarúa transformed Heiséi ni into the green iguana and forced him to hide in the trees and eat only fruit and flowers. With a timid animal back at the bottom of the land's chain of life, the earth's harmony was restored.

GLOSSARY

adaptations – changes in a species that help it survive in a changed environment

aquatic – living or growing in water

captive-breeding – being bred and raised in a place from which escape is not possible

climate change – the gradual increase in Earth's temperature that causes changes in the planet's atmosphere, environments, and long-term weather conditions

clutch – a group of eggs produced and incubated at one time

cultural – of or relating to particular groups in a society that share behaviors and characteristics that are accepted as normal by that group

esophagus – the muscular tube that runs from the back of the mouth to the start of the digestive system

evolved – gradually developed into a new form

extinction – the act or process of becoming extinct; coming to an end or dying out

feral – in a wild state after having been domesticated

hibernate – to spend the winter in a sleep-like state in which breathing and heart rate slow down

hormone – a chemical substance produced in the body that controls and regulates the activity of certain cells and organs

incubated – having kept an egg warm and protected until it is time for it to hatch

indigenous – originating in a particular region or country

Mesoamerica – the area from central Mexico through Central America, including Belize, El Salvador, Guatemala, and Honduras

mythology – a collection of myths, or popular, traditional beliefs or stories that explain how something came to be or that are associated with a person or object

nutrients – substances that give an animal energy and help it grow

paleontologists – people who study fossils of animals, plants, and other organisms that existed long ago

superstitions – beliefs or behaviors that result from misconceptions or faith in magic

SELECTED BIBLIOGRAPHY

Alberts, Allison C., Ronald L. Carter, William K. Hayes, and Emília P. Martins, eds. *Iguanas: Biology and Conservation*. Berkeley: University of California Press, 2004.

Durrell Wildlife Conservation Trust. "Lesser Antillean Iguana." http://www.durrell.org/animals/reptiles/lesser -antillean-iguana/.

Fife, Jerry D. *Iguanas: A Pictorial Guide to Iguanas of the World and Their Care in Captivity*. Ada, Okla.: Living Art Publishing, 2010.

San Diego Zoo. "Animals: Iguana." http://animals .sandiegozoo.org/animals/iguana.

San Diego Zoo Global. "Wildlife Conservancy: Conservation of Caribbean Iguanas." http://www.sandiegozooglobal.org /what_we_do/restoring_nature/caribbean_iguanas_get _head_start/.

Smithsonian National Zoological Park. "Reptiles & Amphibians: Fact Sheets; Green Iguana." http://nationalzoo.si.edu/Animals /ReptilesAmphibians/Facts/FactSheets/Greeniguana.cfm.

Note: Every effort has been made to ensure that any websites listed above were active at the time of publication. However, because of the nature of the Internet, it is impossible to guarantee that these sites will remain active indefinitely or that their contents will not be altered.

Though iguanas may balance on their tails to reach food, they cannot walk on their hind legs.

INDEX

chuckwallas 10, 11, 12, 21, 31, 32, 33

conservation measures 7, 38, 40, 41, 42, 43
    Blue Iguana Recovery Program 41
    protected areas 7, 38, 40, 41, 42, 43
    by zoos and aquariums 43

cultural influences 29–31, 33–35, 44
    ancient artwork 29, 31
    comics 33, 34
    Godzilla 34–35
    mythologies 29, 30–31, 44
    on *The Simpsons* 33
    superstitions 29

desert iguanas 10, 11, 12

eggs 16, 23–24, 29, 42
    and nests 23, 24, 29

Fiji iguanas 10, 11, 12, 24, 26–27, 30
    Fiji crested iguanas 30

food 7, 8, 12, 17, 19, 27, 39
    cacti 12
    flowers 17
    fruit 7, 8, 17
    other plant matter 17, 19

Galápagos land iguanas 10, 11–12, 34

Galápagos marine iguanas 10, 11, 12, 16, 17, 21, 26, 38, 39–40

green iguanas 7–8, 10, 11, 12, 16, 19, 21, 23, 26, 31, 42

habitats 7, 10, 11–12, 21, 29, 31, 34, 37, 38, 39, 40, 41, 42, 43, 44
    Central America 7, 10, 12, 31, 41, 42, 43
    deserts 10, 12, 21, 31, 37
    forests 10, 12
    islands 10, 11–12, 29, 34, 38, 39, 40, 41, 42, 43
    loss of 41, 43
    mangrove swamps 11
    North America 10, 12, 21, 29, 31, 42
    rainforests 37
    South America 10, 11, 12, 31, 38, 44
    volcanoes 34

hatchlings 24

hibernating 21

Iguanidae family 11, 16

life expectancy 21

mating 21–23, 26, 27, 42
    courtship rituals 22
    and periphery and sneaker males 22–23

physical characteristics 7, 12, 15, 16, 17, 19, 21, 22, 23, 24, 26, 27, 30, 34, 39, 40
    body temperature 12, 15, 19
    claws 7, 16, 23
    colors 15, 24, 26, 27, 30, 34
    dewlaps 15, 22, 27
    differences between males and females 15, 16, 24
    digestive systems 19
    dorsal crests 15
    femoral pores 15, 16, 21, 24
    jowls 15, 16, 24
    sizes 15, 16, 21, 39, 40
    spines 15
    tails 15, 16, 27
    teeth 17, 19, 27
    tongues 12, 19, 27

populations 11, 12, 29, 30, 40, 41, 42
    endangered species 11, 29, 30, 41, 42

predators 19, 24, 27, 29, 42, 43
    hawks 27
    introduced animals 29, 42, 43

relationship with humans 12, 31, 33, 41, 42
    as food 31, 33, 42
    as pets 12, 42

relatives 11, 12, 16–17, 24, 29, 37
    ancestors 11, 37
    other reptiles 11, 16, 24, 37

rock iguanas 10, 11, 12, 16, 21, 23, 27, 29, 41–42
    Andros Island iguanas 29
    Grand Cayman blue iguanas 16, 23, 41–42
    rhinoceros iguanas 21, 27
    White Cay iguanas 42

scientific research 37, 38–40
    by Charles Darwin 38

skin shedding 24, 26

social groups 15, 21–22, 23, 27, 37
    colonies 21
    and communication 15, 27
    and scent marking 21, 22

spiny-tailed iguanas 10, 11, 12, 16, 41
    Roatán spiny-tailed iguanas 41
    Utila spiny-tailed iguanas 11
    Yucatán spiny-tailed iguanas 16

swimming 21, 38

threats 42–43